LOUIS PASTEUR

Nina Morgan

The Bookwright Press
New York · 1992

Pioneers of Science *Pasteur*

Archimedes

Alexander Graham Bell

Karl Benz

Marie Curie

Thomas Edison

Albert Einstein

Michael Faraday

Galileo

Guglielmo Marconi

Isaac Newton

Louis Pasteur

Leonardo da Vinci

First published in the
United States in 1992 by
The Bookwright Press
387 Park Avenue South
New York, NY 10016

First published in 1991 by
Wayland (Publishers) Ltd
61 Western Road, Hove
East Sussex BN3 1JD, England

© Copyright 1991 Wayland (Publishers) Limited

Library of Congress Cataloging-in-Publication Data
Nina Morgan.
  Louis Pasteur / by Nina Morgan.
    p. cm.—(Pioneers of science)
  Includes index.
  Summary: Discusses the life and work of Louis Pasteur with
emphasis on the importance of his scientific discoveries.
    ISBN 0–531–18459–5
  1. Pasteur, Louis 1822–1895—Biography—Juvenile literature.
2. Science—History—Juvenile literature. 3. Scientists—France—
Biography—Juvenile literature. 4. Microbiologists—France—
Biography—Juvenile literature. [1. Pasteur, Louis, 1822–1895.
2. Scientists.] I. Title. II. Series.
Q143.P2M38 1992
509.2—dc20
[B]   91–16935
                                                   CIP
                                                   AC

Typeset by DP Press Ltd, Sevenoaks, Kent
Printed in Italy by Rotolito Lombardo S.p.A.

Contents

1 The World before Pasteur   4
2 The Shy Artist   7
3 Chemicals, Crystals and Light   11
4 Microbes and Fermentation   18
5 Savior of the Silkworm Industry   25
6 Conquering Diseases   32
7 Legacy for the Future   42
Date Chart   46
Glossary   47
Books to Read   47
Index   48

In 1822, when Louis Pasteur was born in a small town in the Jura mountains in the eastern part of France, hospitals were terrifying places. More often than not, going to the hospital for an operation meant a death sentence. No one realized that tiny microbes, or germs, were responsible for infections, and as a result, diseases spread through hospitals like wildfire.

Outside life was not much better. In the crowded slums of the big cities hundreds of thousands of people died of epidemic diseases such as cholera and typhoid. Mothers died in childbirth, and many children did not survive beyond infancy. Because doctors did not understand what caused diseases and infections, they had no way of preventing them.

Crowded and unhealthy conditions in city slums provided fertile ground for epidemic diseases. Because no one understood the causes of these diseases, it was impossible to prevent their spread.

Pasteur was the first person to understand the connection between microbes and disease. Through his work in developing vaccines, children can now be inoculated to protect them against many common diseases such as diphtheria, measles and whooping cough.

People had known of the existence of microbes ever since the Dutch scientist Anton van Leeuwenhoek had invented the microscope in the late 1600s. But no one understood how microbes arrived in the first place or how they reproduced themselves. Pasteur believed that if he made a thorough study of microbes he might be able to understand their role in disease.

Although other scientists had studied diseases before Pasteur, none had been able to make the connection with microbes. But, as he once said, "chance favors the prepared mind." Pasteur's careful experiments finally proved once and for all that microbes can be passed to people and animals in the water they drink, the foods they eat and the air they breathe. This breakthrough led to the idea that microbes could be controlled and that, by means of vaccination, it was possible to prevent them from taking hold in the first place.

Thanks to the unending curiosity and patient experimentation of Louis Pasteur, the sciences of microbiology and immunology were born, and the causes, control and prevention of diseases began to be understood. Many diseases that once killed thousands of people can now be prevented by vaccination. Thanks to Louis Pasteur, hospitals are now places where people go to get well, rather than to die.

In the nineteenth century, hospitals were dangerous, unhealthy places. Thanks to the work of Pasteur, we now understand the importance of hygiene in preventing the spread of diseases. Today hospitals are clean, healthy places where people go to get well.

2 The Shy Artist

Jean Joseph Pasteur and his wife, Jeanne Etiennette, had a special reason to celebrate the Christmas season of 1822. On December 27, just two days after the holiday, their second child, Louis, was born in their tiny house on the Rue de Tanneurs in Dôle, France. Like the rest of their neighbors, the Pasteurs lived in a tannery. Jean Joseph supported his family by turning the fresh skins of cattle and sheep into leather.

The Rue de Tanneurs is now called the Rue de Pasteur, but Louis did not live there for long. When he was three his family moved to the small town of Arbois, about 15 miles to the southwest. Louis and his older sister were soon joined by two younger sisters.

The Pasteurs' house in the village of Arbois in eastern France. The house had pits dug in the yard, which Louis' father used in his work as a tanner.

Pasteur's portrait of his mother. His family and friends and the surrounding countryside were among his favorite subjects for his paintings.

Louis's first school was the Ecole Primaire in Arbois. Louis enjoyed his school days, but he was not a remarkable student. He was quiet and shy, enjoyed playing with his school friends and liked to go fishing. He also loved to draw and paint portraits of his family and friends and the countryside around him.

Louis was a careful and cautious thinker, and was not considered to be particularly intelligent by most of his teachers. But one of his schoolmasters did realize that Louis was cut out for better things. He thought Louis should become a teacher, and persuaded Jean Joseph to send his son to Paris to study for entrance to the Ecole Normale Supérieure, a training college in Paris.

In 1838, when he was sixteen, Louis went to Paris to study. But it was not a happy time. After six weeks, he became so homesick that his father hurried to Paris to bring him back home.

In spite of his difficult time in Paris, Louis did not give up the idea of entering school there. In 1839, he went to study at the Royal College at Besançon, only 25 miles away from his family. There he was happy, and in 1840, when he was eighteen, he was awarded the degree of Bachelor of Letters. After his exams, Louis was offered a post at Besançon as a junior teacher. He could not believe his luck. "I assure you I am not really worth it," he wrote to his parents. But happy as he was in his new role, he still hoped to return to Paris, where, as he said, "study is deeper."

In 1842 Louis took the examination for entrance to the Ecole Normale Supérieure. Although he passed the examination, he was placed only 15th out of 22 candidates, and he received a mediocre result in the chemistry examination. Louis wanted to do better and decided to study in Paris again. In 1842 Louis and a childhood friend, Louis Chappuis, moved to Paris where Pasteur entered the Barbet Pension (a boarding school), where Monsieur Barbet had agreed to reduce Louis' fees in exchange for his teaching some of the younger pupils. Louis soon made himself so useful that Monsieur Barbet canceled his fees entirely.

The entrance to the Ecole Normale Supérieure in Paris. Louis entered the Ecole as a student in 1843. In 1857 he returned there as Director of Scientific Studies.

All this hard work paid off because when Louis took the examination for entrance to the Ecole Normale a second time, in 1843, he came in fourth out of all the candidates and received prizes in physics. Louis was so eager to begin his studies in Paris that he arrived a few days before the other students and had to spend his first nights sleeping in an empty dormitory.

Jean Joseph was delighted by his son's accomplishments and his enthusiasm for his work, but he also worried that Louis might overwork. He wrote to Chappuis: "Do tell Louis not to work so much; it is not good to strain one's brain." However, not even the pleas of his father and his friend could prevent Louis from immersing himself in his work and making the most of his studies in Paris.

The Library of the Ecole Normale Supérieure. During his time at the Ecole, Louis spent many happy hours reading here.

3 Chemistry, Crystals and Light

The first subject to grip Pasteur's imagination was chemistry. Attending chemistry lectures was not enough for him; he insisted on proving the theories for himself in the laboratory.

Pasteur loved his time at the Ecole Normale. By the time he was twenty-five years old, in 1847, he had qualified as a doctor of science and become fascinated with the chemistry of crystals. These beautiful objects appealed to his artistic nature, and they offered tremendous possibilities for scientific research. There were so many questions to answer!

While at the Ecole Normale, Pasteur made important discoveries about the structure of crystals. In 1849 he moved to Strasbourg, where he met Marie Laurent, who later became his wife.

Crystals

Crystals are common in nature and come in all shapes and sizes. Many substances, including sugar and salt, form crystals. Every crystal is bounded by definite faces, which intersect at characteristic angles. The shape of a crystal is governed by the three-dimensional arrangement of the atoms or molecules that make up the crystal.

It is possible to learn something about a crystal's atomic structure by studying the way light is scattered through it. This, in turn, gives valuable clues as to how the substance that makes up the crystal will react chemically.

A thin slice of sodium sulfate crystals shown under a polarizing light microscope, in which the light rays travel in only one plane. The beautiful colors and shapes of the crystals seen under polarized light give valuable clues to their atomic structure.

Pasteur began by studying dimorphous compounds, crystals that crystallize in two different shapes. He then became interested in the crystals of tartaric acid, which occur in the encrustation, or "tartar," that forms on the insides of wine barrels.

Although all the crystals in the tartar appeared to have the same shape and chemical composition, chemists had noted that light behaves oddly when it travels through different solutions of the crystals dissolved in water. In some solutions the light is bent as it travels through. But in other solutions light travels straight through. No one understood why this should happen, and no one could predict which solution would bend the light. Pasteur was determined to find the answer to this puzzle.

He began by examining tartaric acid crystals through a magnifying glass. The work was tedious and seemed to be leading nowhere. Then one day he noticed that on some crystals one of the faces sloped in one direction, but the same face on other crystals sloped in the opposite direction. When Pasteur made separate solutions of each type of crystal in water, he found that in one solution a beam of light was bent to the right, but in the other the light was bent to the left. When the solutions were combined, the bending of the light to the right canceled out the bending to the left, and the light traveled straight through.

Pasteur was so excited by his discovery he rushed out of his laboratory and embraced the first person he saw. His experiment had not only shown him the difference between the two types of tartaric acid crystals, it had also proved it was possible to study the structure of a crystal by seeing what happened to light as it traveled through the crystal or a solution of crystals. In fact, Pasteur had opened up a whole new branch of chemistry – the science of stereochemistry.

Pasteur's joy at his first important discovery turned to sadness when his mother died suddenly in May 1848. At first he was too upset to continue with his work, and he went back to Arbois. But in September, he returned to Paris and asked the famous physicist Jean-Baptiste Biot to verify his work on tartaric acid crystals. Biot carefully repeated the experiments and found, like Pasteur, that the right-handed crystals bent light to the right and the left-handed crystals bent light to the left.

Biot was so moved by Pasteur's discovery that he said "this touches my very heart." Biot then went on to offer help and support to Pasteur and to spread the word about his new discovery to the Academy of Sciences in Paris.

In January 1849, at the age of twenty-six, Pasteur was given his first important job – as a lecturer in chemistry at the University of Strasbourg. He had not been in Strasbourg very long before he met and fell in love with Marie Laurent, the daughter of the university principal.

Jean-Baptiste Biot, the famous physicist who verified Pasteur's work on left- and right-handed crystals. Biot, who had done important work toward the understanding of the way light travels through crystals, became a great supporter of the young Pasteur.

Within fifteen days Pasteur asked Marie to marry him. He wrote to her father that "all I possess is good health, a willing spirit and my work," and he begged Marie "not to be hasty in your judgement of me . . . Time will show you that, under a cold and shy outside, which

15

A view of the city of Strasbourg. Pasteur spent five happy and productive years in Strasbourg, working on crystals and lecturing in chemistry at the university there.

doubtless displeases you, there is a heart full of affection for you."

The couple were married on May 29, 1849, and Marie devoted herself to helping her husband. She took great interest in Pasteur's work, and their discussions together often inspired him with new ideas. In 1850 their daughter, Jeanne, was born; she was later followed by a son, Jean-Baptiste, and another daughter, Cécile.

Pasteur's years at Strasbourg were happy and productive. He continued to study tartaric acid and handedness in molecules. His work created such interest and excitement that in 1853 a whole sitting of the Academy of Sciences was devoted to discussing it, and the French government awarded him the Legion of Honor for his achievements in chemistry. He was also awarded several other prizes for his scientific achievements. These awards only served to make Pasteur more determined than ever to continue his research. He spent much of the money he received on new instruments and salaries for his laboratory technicians.

In September 1854 Pasteur was offered a new challenge. He was appointed Professor of Chemistry and Dean of the Faculty of Science at the University of Lille, in northern France. Lille was a center for the fermentation of beets to make alcohol, and from the moment he arrived in Lille, Pasteur became interested in the problems of fermentation. After all, as he once said in a public lecture, "who would not be interested if you gave him a potato and told him from that potato you can make sugar, from sugar you can make alcohol and from alcohol vinegar?"

Louis and Marie Pasteur. Marie devoted herself to helping her husband. Pasteur often discussed his work with her, and she gave him inspiration for new experiments.

4

Microbes and Fermentation

Pasteur began his new teaching duties with great enthusiasm. His lectures were interesting and exciting, and the lecture hall was always crowded. He delighted in taking his pupils off on tours of the factories and metal works of the region, so that they could see chemistry in action for themselves.

The new young professor was also happy to give advice to local farmers about fertilizers and manures. But one day in 1856, Monsieur Bigo, the

Huge wooden vats used for the fermentation of beet juice to make alcohol. When Pasteur arrived in Lille in 1854, the alcohol manufacturers asked him to solve the problem of alcohol souring in the vats.

Pasteur at work in his laboratory.

father of one of his pupils and the owner of a large factory manufacturing alcohol from beet juice, came to him with a puzzling and interesting problem. The juice in the vats often turned sour. This spoiling was costing Monsieur Bigo thousands of francs a day – and he wanted to find out why.

This was just the sort of problem that Pasteur enjoyed tackling. His first step was to visit Monsieur Bigo's factory and take samples of the liquid from the successfully fermenting vats, along with samples of the slimy liquid from the soured vats. When he examined the fermenting juice under his microscope he saw thousands of tiny yeast cells. Scientists knew that yeast cells were always present in fermenting liquors, but no one knew what effect they had. When Pasteur looked at the yeast cells he noticed that they were alive.

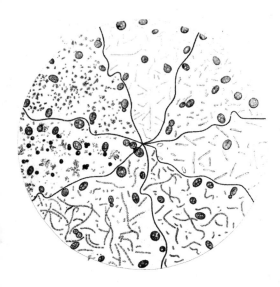

Pasteur's drawing of the tiny cells and rods of living organisms that he saw in fermenting juices. Some, such as the round yeast cells, are responsible for fermentation, but others, such as the various rod-shaped bacteria, cause the liquor to spoil.

Suddenly he understood how fermentation took place. When the yeast cells grew and divided, they gave off alcohol and a clear gas called carbon dioxide.

When Pasteur peered at a drop of liquid from the sour vats, he did not see any yeast cells. Instead, the liquid was swarming with millions of minute wriggling bacteria, which looked like tiny black rods. Pasteur developed a theory to explain what was happening. The bacteria had overrun the yeast cells, and instead of producing alcohol and carbon dioxide, they were producing lactic acid, the acid that sours milk.

Pasteur tested his theory by placing the growing bacteria in some soup made from yeast cells. He repeated his experiment several times until he was absolutely sure. The black rods were living bacteria, and these tiny microbes were producing lactic acid, which spoiled alcohol and milk.

Although he could not yet tell Monsieur Bigo how to kill off the microbes in his vats, he was able to tell him how to ensure that good alcohol would be produced. If even one bacterium was found in the vat of juice, the whole vat had to be discarded. The fermenting industry in Lille was saved, and Pasteur became a local hero.

His work on fermenting beet juice convinced Pasteur that microbes must be at the heart of many other chemical processes. Perhaps they even caused diseases. He was determined to find out.

In 1857 Pasteur was called back to the Ecole Normale in Paris to become the Administrator and Director of Scientific Studies. It was there that his daughter Marie-Louise was born, in 1858. In 1859 his oldest daughter, Jeanne, died suddenly from typhoid fever, when she was only nine years old. Her death saddened Pasteur, but it also made him more determined than ever to find out everything he could about microbes.

In order to show that spoilage is caused by airborne organisms, Pasteur used a series of flasks with S-shaped necks, which trapped dust and microbes. Pasteur showed that as long as the liquid in the flasks was kept out of the necks, and not exposed to microbes, it remained clear and did not spoil.

Pasteur's work in Monsieur Bigo's factory had convinced him that microbes were carried in the air and reproduced by cell division. But his views were not shared by most other scientists. They believed that microbes simply appeared as if by magic – the result of spontaneous generation.

Pasteur set out to devise an experiment to prove his theory. He made a soup out of yeast and placed it in flasks that had long S-shaped necks. He first boiled the yeast soup in the flasks to kill any organisms it contained. As the soup cooled, air was drawn into the flasks, but any particles, such as dust or microbes, were trapped in the necks of the flasks. The necks were then tightly sealed.

Next he shook some of the flasks so that the liquid went into the necks and was contaminated by the dust and microbes trapped in the bend. The liquid in these flasks soon became cloudy and filled with millions of microbes. But the liquid in flasks that had been kept upright, so that the liquid did not come into contact with the microbes trapped in the neck, remained perfectly clear and free of organisms. These flasks are still kept at the Pasteur Institute in Paris, and still contain clear microbe-free liquid, more than 130 years after Pasteur carried out his experiment.

While experimenting with his flasks, Pasteur found that some of the microbes were anaerobic: they could grow only in the absence of air. In 1860 he reported his results to the Academy of Sciences and suggested that microbes might be the cause of many serious diseases. Clearly more research was needed.

The wine industry was one of France's most important industries. Pasteur's researches into microbes and fermentation in wine led to many improvements.

Pasteurization

In the process of pasteurization, the liquid being treated is heated to a temperature high enough to kill the germs, but not so high that it spoils the taste of the liquid. The temperature and length of time needed vary with different liquids. Much of the milk we drink and the milk products we eat today are pasteurized to make sure they are free of germs.
(Below) Bottles containing milk that has been pasteurized have sterilized tops put on them before they are sold to the public.

In 1862 Pasteur was elected to membership of the Academy of Sciences. The next year he was appointed to be the Professor of Geology, Physics and Chemistry at the School of Fine Arts in Paris. He also celebrated the birth of his daughter Camille. Pasteur's work on microbes and fermentation was now becoming very well known. Even the Emperor Napoleon III became interested, and he asked Pasteur to study the diseases of wine.

Pasteur's apparatus for cooling the fermented juice in the wine-making process.

In 1864 Pasteur fulfilled the Emperor's request. He traveled to his home town of Arbois to investigate the problems of the local winemakers, who were having great problems with wine turning sour or tasting bitter. Once again Pasteur was able to show that microbes were the cause.

By careful experimentation Pasteur worked out the process of pasteurization, a method to kill the microbes in wine. Soon it was discovered that pasteurization could also be used to kill the microbes in beer and milk and to keep them disease free and fresh for longer. What started as an investigation into the problems of a group of local winemakers turned out to be a great breakthrough for public health.

5

Savior of the Silkworm Industry

Pasteur's work on the role of microbes in fermentation and in the spoiling of wine gave support to his idea that it might be possible to control diseases by controlling the micro-organisms that caused them. But first a lot more work had to be done to prove that the germ theory of disease was correct.

Pasteur soon had an opportunity to test his theory. The silkworm growers in southern France were in trouble. In 1849 silkworms had begun to die in large numbers. The disease spread quickly, and by 1864 silkworms as far away as China were being infected. Pasteur decided to travel to southern France to see what he could do.

The interior of a French magnanerie, a house for raising silkworms.

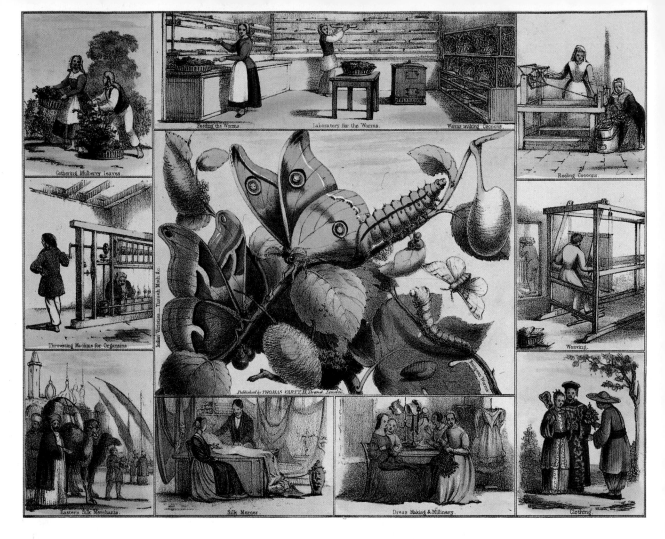

In 1865 Pasteur arrived in Alès, one of the centers of the silkworm industry in southern France. He studied thousands of silkworm chrysalids and moths under his microscope and thought he could recognize the diseased insects by the presence of little globules that looked like grains of pepper. He believed that mature silk moths that had the disease passed it on to their offspring in their eggs. Therefore, he hoped to control the disease by convincing breeders to destroy all the eggs from infected moths.

While he waited for the new crop of silkworm eggs to hatch, Pasteur returned to Paris, where tragedy struck. His youngest daughter, Camille, died. Then, in 1866, his twelve-year-old daughter, Cécile, died of typhoid fever. Pasteur was a very sad man when he returned to Alès.

An illustration published in 1850 showing the process of silk production, from the silkworm to the finished product. Crysalids, silkworms and moths, the three stages in the life of a silkworm, are shown in the central picture.

News about the silkworms was not good either. The worms hatching from the eggs laid by seemingly healthy moths turned out to have the disease. The silkworm breeders were very bitter, and Pasteur felt responsible for their plight. Pasteur worked even harder than ever, and eventually he discovered that the epidemic was caused by two diseases, rather than one. He showed that both the diseases were hereditary and contagious. Not only could the microbes that caused the diseases be passed on in the silkworm eggs, but healthy silkworms could also become infected by eating contaminated food. Once he understood how the diseases were caused, he was able to recommend to the breeders how they could be controlled. The silkworm industry was saved!

In 1867 Pasteur returned to Paris where he was appointed Professor of Chemistry at the Sorbonne. He was also awarded the Grand Prize medal at the Universal Exhibition in Paris for his work on pasteurization.

The Sorbonne in Paris. Pasteur returned to this famous university to become Professor of Chemistry in 1867.

News of Pasteur's work was not confined to France. In Scotland, the Professor of Surgery in Glasgow, a surgeon named Joseph Lister, was following Pasteur's discoveries with great interest. In 1865 Lister realized that Pasteur's germ theory of disease showed that the infections that killed so many people after operations were the result of microbes carried in the air or on the hands or instruments of the surgeons. This led him to develop the method of antiseptic surgery, a method in which the operating theaters, hands and clothing of the doctors, and the patient's wound are all sterilized to kill microbes. Thousands of lives were saved as a result, and Lister wrote to Pasteur to thank him for "furnishing me with the principles upon which alone the antiseptic system can be carried out."

Joseph Lister, photographed in a hospital ward in London. He followed Pasteur's work on microbes with great interest, using it as a basis for his development of antiseptic surgery, which saved many lives.

The Hungarian doctor and scientist Ignaz Philipp Semmelweiss, who applied Pasteur's germ theory and Lister's antiseptic methods to childbirth.

The Hungarian scientist Ignaz Semmelweiss had years earlier applied antiseptic methods to childbirth. The work of Pasteur, Lister and Semmelweiss probably saved more lives than all the scientific discoveries that had been made before them.

In 1868, Pasteur himself was able to benefit from the improved conditions in hospitals. On the day he was due to read a paper at the Academy of Sciences he suffered a stroke. At the age of forty-five, he suddenly found himself partially paralyzed. No one expected Pasteur to live, much less to carry on his work, but he was determined to go on. Just three months later he traveled back to southern France, and later to the Villa Vincentina near Trieste, to continue his work on silkworm diseases. In 1870 Pasteur returned to Paris, but was soon forced to leave for the relative safety of his childhood home in Arbois when the Franco-Prussian war broke out.

Pasteur's apparatus for cooling and fermenting the liquid used in beer-making. The apparatus included a small window in the top so that the progress of the brew could be checked. A jacket of cold water, supplied via the pipe labeled "M," was used to keep the vessel cool.

In 1871 Pasteur visited London for the first time and undertook a study of beer production. As he had found with wine and vinegar, he was able to show that spoilage of beer was due to microbes. The more he studied the various types of fermentation, the more he became convinced that there was a link between fermentation problems and diseases in humans and animals. He felt certain that microbes were the cause of disease. But the problem was how to prove it.

In 1876 the proof was found by a Prussian doctor named Robert Koch. Koch spent three years studying the cattle disease anthrax. After examining thousands of slides under a microscope and conducting hundreds of tests, Koch was able to come up with a method for proving that a specific microbe causes a specific disease.

By using his method Koch proved Pasteur's theory to be right: one microbe for one disease. The next step was to learn how to control the microbe.

Pasteur began his attack on disease-causing microbes with a study of the cattle disease anthrax. The disease was ruining agriculture in France. Cattle that contracted anthrax usually died within a few hours. People were also susceptible to this terrible disease. Even a pinprick or a scratch was enough to pass on the deadly microbe. The disease spread away from farms via infected meat or furs. Most people who caught the disease died from it. But occasionally there were people and animals who survived. These survivors turned out to hold the key to control of the disease, but Pasteur did not realize this at first.

When Pasteur and his assistants began studying anthrax bacteria they took a great personal risk. Any cut or scratch that brought them into contact with infected blood could prove deadly. At the same time Pasteur began studying other types of infections such as childbed fever and chicken cholera.

Following on from the work of Robert Koch, Pasteur isolated the chicken cholera microbe obtained from the body of an infected chicken. He then grew the microbe in a laboratory culture and injected some of the resulting microbes into healthy chicks. The chicks soon developed the disease and died.

One day Pasteur discovered an old culture that had been forgotten in a cupboard for several weeks. To his surprise, he found that when he inoculated healthy chicks with this old culture, they became ill but did not die. He later inoculated these same chicks with a fresh culture of

Opposite *Work on animals, including rabbits, chickens and dogs, helped Pasteur to develop his ideas about the germ theory of disease and to test the effectiveness of vaccines.*

the microbe and discovered that the chicks had developed a resistance to the disease. The disease did not kill them.

Pasteur was elated. He realized that it could be possible to prevent many other types of diseases by vaccinating people and animals with weak cultures of the specific disease-causing microbes.

Pasteur carrying out an experiment in his laboratory.

The weakened microbes caused a resistance to the disease to be built up, and this resistance provided protection against infection. He began by developing a weakened culture, or vaccine, of anthrax bacteria.

Once his vaccine was developed Pasteur was so sure that it would be successful that he decided to test it in public, even though failure would be very humiliating. In 1881 he began a trial using fifty sheep and ten cows. Twenty-five of the sheep and six of the cows were vaccinated, using a weakened form of the anthrax bacterium. Each animal was vaccinated twice at intervals of fifteen days. Another twenty-five sheep and the remaining four cows, along with the original vaccinated group of animals, were then all inoculated with the deadly anthrax virus.

A sheep being vaccinated against the deadly disease anthrax in 1882, just one year after Pasteur had developed a successful vaccine using a weakened form of anthrax bacteria.

The vaccinated and unvaccinated animals were placed in separate fields, and the anxious wait began. But it was not long before Pasteur found out that he had been successful. After two days, all of the unvaccinated animals had died of anthrax, and all of the vaccinated ones had survived. When Pasteur arrived to inspect the results of his trial the farmers greeted him with cheers. Anthrax was conquered at last.

After his triumph with the anthrax vaccine, honors were showered on Pasteur. In 1881 he was awarded the Grand Cross of the Legion of Honor, and in 1882 he was elected to the French Academy. When he visited London to represent France at the International Medical Congress delegates from all over the world cheered when he entered the hall.

In spite of his many honors and great fame, Pasteur was not a man to allow triumph to go to his head. He became convinced that vaccines against

In 1881 Pasteur was awarded the Grand Cross of the Legion of Honor for his work on vaccines.

Rabbits proved to be valuable allies in Pasteur's fight against the dreaded disease, rabies. He used the dried brains of rabbits that had died of rabies to make a vaccine against the disease.

infection were the best hope of conquering disease. "When meditating over a disease, I never think of finding a remedy for it, but instead search for a means to prevent it," he said. In 1883 he developed a vaccine against the serious pig disease, swine fever. He also began studying rabies, a deadly and much feared disease in humans and animals.

Rabies is an inflammation of the brain that causes its victims to become very excitable. The disease affects foxes, wolves, dogs, cats and other carnivores. It is easily transmitted to other animals or to humans by contact with a sick animal's saliva. Victims feel as if they are being strangled and eventually die from suffocation or become paralyzed. Sufferers are thirsty, but spasms make them unable to swallow water. Rabid animals act in a wild manner and often foam at the mouth. Recovery is very rare.

When Pasteur began his work on rabies it had already been discovered that the microbe that caused the disease was present in the saliva of its victims. Because madness is one of the symptoms of rabies, Pasteur reasoned that the microbe must attack the central nervous system. He first studied the saliva of animals and humans who had died of rabies and confirmed the presence of a specific microbe, too small to be seen through a microscope, which we now call a virus. He then examined tissue from the brain and spinal cords of some of the victims and deduced the presence of the virus there too. Pasteur thought it would be

Pasteur experimenting on a chloroformed rabbit during his search for a cure for rabies.

A vaccine against rabies

Pasteur set about making his vaccine by drying part of the brain of a rabbit that had died of rabies in a sterilized vial for fourteen days. The drying weakened the virus so much that it could not cause rabies. He used the weakened virus to make a vaccine, which he tested on dogs. First he injected an extract of the dried brain into the dogs. When they did not develop rabies he injected them with the extract of a brain of a rabid rabbit, which was dried for just thirteen days. He continued his trials by injecting dogs with extracts of brains of rabid animals, which had been dried for shorter and shorter times. None of the dogs developed rabies. (Below) The laboratory kennels housing dogs used by Pasteur in his experiments to find a rabies vaccine.

Kennels housed laboratory dogs that were used by Pasteur in his experiments to find a vaccine against rabies.

possible to make a vaccine using weakened strains of the disease-causing organism (attenuated vaccine) from a weakened strain of the virus.

At last Pasteur was satisfied that he could prevent the dreaded disease in dogs, but he did not dare test the drug on a human volunteer. If Pasteur's rabies vaccine was found to be too strong for use in humans, trials using healthy people could result in their catching the dreaded disease.

But on July 6, 1885, the decision to carry out a human trial was made for him. A nine-year-old boy, Joseph Meister, was brought to him by his distraught mother. Joseph had been bitten many times by a rabid dog two days before, and she begged Pasteur to try to save her son. If the vaccine failed, Pasteur knew he would be blamed for Joseph's death. But if Pasteur did nothing, Joseph was likely to die anyway. It was a terrible dilemma for Pasteur, but he decided the vaccine was Joseph's only hope.

Pasteur injected the vaccine into Joseph twelve times over the course of ten days. Joseph's bites healed, and he went home several days after the treatment without having contracted rabies. Young Joseph felt he owed his life to Pasteur and when he grew up he became the gatekeeper at the Pasteur Institute, where he took special care of Pasteur's tomb.

The news of the cure flashed throughout Europe, and victims of bites from rabid animals flooded into Paris to receive Pasteur's treatment.

Pasteur had successfully developed a vaccine for use in humans from one made for animals. The development of the rabies vaccine has saved thousands of lives, and it showed the way for the development of vaccines against many other diseases. Pasteur had won the battle against rabies and was well on the way to winning the war against other disease-causing microbes.

Opposite *Pasteur's pupil, Emile Roux, inoculating a boy against rabies at the Pasteur Institute.*

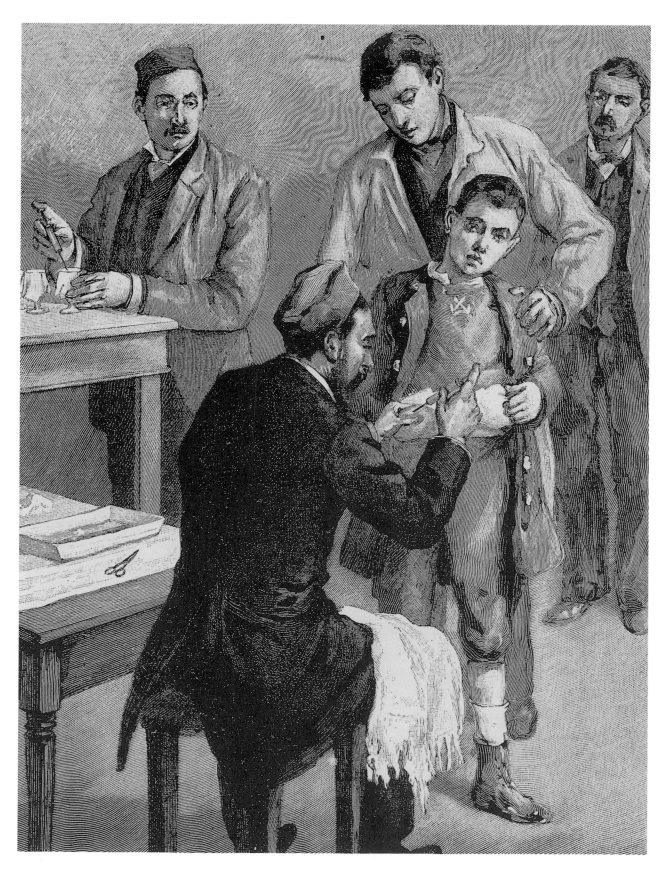

7 Legacy for the Future

The Pasteur Institute in Paris, now a world-renowned center for work on prevention of diseases.

After Pasteur's triumph against rabies, the Academy of Sciences decided to set up a special institute in Paris, to be known as the Pasteur Institute, to organize treatment against the disease. In 1886 they asked for donations, and money poured in from all over the world. The Institute was officially opened in 1888, and Pasteur moved into a large, well-equipped laboratory there.

The work of the institute was soon extended to other fields of microbiology. Today, the Pasteur Institute in Paris is renowned for the important work done there on the prevention of microbial diseases and is well respected for the excellence of its research.

In spite of his increasing age and poor health, Pasteur still continued his research and attended many meetings where he knew his presence would help and encourage younger scientists. As Pasteur's seventieth birthday approached in 1892, committees were set up in various countries to organize events to honor him.

Pasteur at the age of seventy-one with his grandson.

On the morning of his birthday the Great Hall of the Sorbonne in Paris was crowded with delegates who had come to extend their good wishes and express their gratitude for all he had done. Joseph Lister, the British doctor who had saved thousand of lives by developing antiseptic surgery, a method based on Pasteur's research into the spread of microbes, was there. When Lister met Pasteur, the two men embraced, and the delegates were very moved to see the friendship and respect that the two great men felt for each other.

In spite of his age, Pasteur's curiosity remained as lively as ever and his mind was as active as when he was young. His first project in his new laboratory at the Pasteur Institute was to supervise work on a vaccine against diphtheria, a disease that killed thousands of children throughout the world every year.

Emile Roux injecting a horse at the Pasteur Institute in the course of work to develop a weakened vaccine against diphtheria. The fight against diphtheria continues, but Pasteur's vaccine has proved useful, both in preventing the disease and in lessening its effects.

The bacterium that causes diphtheria had been discovered by Dr. Edwin Klebs, in Germany in 1883. Pasteur and his assistants were soon able to show that it was a poison, or toxin, that the bacteria produced which actually caused the disease. Therefore, instead of developing a weakened strain of the diphtheria bacterium to use as a vaccine, they concentrated on developing a weakened form of the toxin. They found that, after animals had been injected with this weakened toxin, they produced an antitoxin in their blood, which reduced the effect of the unaltered diphtheria toxin. The weakened toxin vaccine eventually proved to be effective in humans, in either preventing the disease or lessening its effects in those who were already infected. This was the start of the long fight against diphtheria, which continues to this day.

By the end of 1894, Pasteur was beginning to lose his own battle against ill-health. By the spring of 1895 he was so weak he could hardly walk, and on September 28, 1895, he died peacefully at home, surrounded by his family and friends and students. Pasteur had once said to his students "You bring me the deepest joy that can be felt by a man whose invincible belief is that science and peace will triumph over ignorance and war." He died happy in the knowledge that his students, and their students after them, would continue to carry on the fight against disease that he had begun.

A medal struck to commemorate Pasteur's work in the prevention and cure of microbial diseases.

Date Chart

1822 (December 27) Pasteur born in Dôle, France.

1839–42 Studies at the Royal College at Besançon for entrance to the Ecole Normale Supérieure in Paris.

1843 Enters Ecole Normale Supérieure.

1844 Begins chemical and crystallographic studies. Discovers molecular asymmetry.

1849 Appointed Lecturer of Chemistry at Strasbourg University. He marries Marie Laurent, daughter of the university principal.

1854 Appointed Professor of Chemistry and Dean of the new Faculty of Science at Lille University.

1856 Begins study of fermentation.

1857 Becomes Director of Scientific Studies at the Ecole Normale in Paris.

1861 Discovers the existence of anaerobic life.

1864 Invents process of pasteurization.

1865 Begins work on silkworm diseases.

1867 Appointed Professor of Chemistry at the Sorbonne in Paris.

1871 Begins studies on beer fermentation.

1877 Starts study of anthrax.

1879 During work on chicken cholera, discovers how to immunize against disease using weakened microbes.

1880 Starts studying rabies.

1881 Demonstrates a successful vaccination against anthrax. Is awarded the Grand Cross of the Legion of Honor.

1885 (July 6) successfully vaccinates Joseph Meister against rabies after he was bitten by a rabid dog.

1888 Pasteur Institute is officially opened.

1894 Pasteur Institute develops a vaccination for diphtheria.

1895 (September 28) Pasteur dies at Villeneuve L'Etang in France.

Books to Read

Bains, Rae. *Louis Pasteur* (Troll Associates, 1985)

Johnson, Spencer. *The Value of Believing in Yourself: The Story of Louis Pasteur* (Oak Tree Publications, 1976)

Rich, Beverly. *Louis Pasteur: The Scientist Who Found the Cause of Infectious Disease and Invented Pasteurization* (Gareth Stevens, 1989)

Sabin, Francene. *Louis Pasteur: Young Scientist* (Troll Associates, 1983)

Picture acknowledgments

Mary Evans Picture Library 4, 14, 18, 19, 27, 29, 31, 33, 34, 37; Hughes-Gilbey Library 7; Mansell Collection 11, 16, 38, 43; Milk Marketing Board 22; Rex Photos 42; Ann Ronan Picture Library 9, 10, 20, 21, 23, 24, 25, 26, 30, 35, 39, 41, 44, 45; Science Photo Library 5, 6, 12, 15; Wayland iii, 8, 17, 28, 36.

Glossary

Anaerobic Able to survive without air. Some anaerobic organisms die if they are exposed to air.

Antiseptic surgery The method of using only microbe-free dressings and equipment in hospitals and when treating wounds.

Bacteria (Bacterium sing.) Microscopic organisms, some of them harmful, which are present everywhere, including in the human body.

Carnivores Animals that eat flesh.

Central nervous system The nerve tissue that coordinates the activities of animals. In humans and other animals with backbones, the central nervous system consists of the brain and the spinal cord.

Chemistry The branch of science concerned with how substances react with other substances.

Compound A substance made up of two or more different elements.

Contagious (of a disease) Capable of being passed on by direct contact with a diseased person or other animal.

Crystal A solid substance with a regular shape, in which plane faces intersect at definite angles. The shape of a crystal is due to the arrangement of the atoms or molecules of which it is made.

Culture The experimental growth of microorganisms.

Dimorphous Something that occurs in two distinct forms or shapes.

Epidemic A widespread occurrence of a disease.

Germ theory of disease The idea that specific diseases are caused by specific microbes.

Hereditary Passed on from parents to offspring.

Immunology The branch of biology involving the study of immunity – the ability of an organism to resist disease.

Microbiology The branch of biology involving the study of microorganisms.

Microbes Tiny forms of life, such as bacteria, which are so small that they can only be seen under a microscope. Many microbes cause diseases.

Organism Any living thing, including animals or plants, bacteria or viruses.

Pasteurization The process for killing harmful microbes in food by heating the food to a certain temperature and keeping it at that temperature for a certain time.

Physics The branch of science concerned with the properties of matter and energy and the relationship between them.

Spontaneous generation The theory that microbes just appeared out of nowhere. The theory led to the idea that microbes did not have a lifecycle and that it was not possible to control their occurrence.

Stereochemistry The study of the arrangement of atoms and molecules in substances. The study of crystals is important in stereochemistry.

Sterilized Treated by heat or chemicals so as to be free from microbes.

Toxin Poison. Antitoxin lessens the effects of the poison. It is produced by the body in response to a toxin.

Vaccine Material derived from disease-causing microbes or their toxins, which are injected into people and animals (vaccination) in order to make them resistant (immune) to the disease.

Index

anthrax 31, 32, 35
antiseptics 28, 29

beets, fermentation of 18
Bigo, M. 19, 20, 21
Biot, Jean-Baptiste 14

Chappuis, Louis 9, 10
chicken cholera 32
crystals 12
  dimorphism of 15

diphtheria 42–3
diseases 4, 5, 6

germ theory of disease 25, 28, 29, 33

hospitals 4, 6

immunology 6

Koch, Robert 31

Leeuwenhoek, Anton van 5
Lister, Joseph 28, 43

Meister, Joseph 40
microbes 4, 5, 20–24, 28, 30–32, 35, 38,
  40
microbiology 6, 41

Napoleon III, Emperor 23

Pasteur, Jean Joseph 7, 8, 11
Pasteur, Louis
  birth 7
  studies at Besançon 9
  enters Ecole Normale Supérieure 9, 10
  qualifies as doctor of science 11
  studies structure of crystals 11,
    13, 14

appointed lecturer at Strasbourg
    University 14, 16
awarded Legion of Honor 16
marriage 16
Professor at Lille University 17
discovers microbes in fermenting
    vinegar 17
Director of Ecole Normale 20
research into microbes 21–3
research into wine spoilage 24
invents pasteurization process 24
researches into silkworm diseases 26–7
Professor at Sorbonne Unversity 27
finds microbes in beer 30
studies disease-causing microbes 32
develops anthrax vaccine 35
awarded Grand Cross of Legion
of Honor 36
begins study of rabies 37
develops rabies vaccine 39–40
successful rabies injection of Joseph
    Meister 40
supervises work on diphtheria
    vaccine 42–4
death 44

Pasteur, Marie 16, 17
Pasteur Institute 42, 43
pasteurization 23, 24

rabies 37, 38, 39
rabies vaccine 37
Roux, Emile 40, 44

Semmelweiss, Ignaz 29
silkworms, disease in 25

vaccination 6, 34, 35

wine industry 22